Dropbox Essentials

The Complete Beginner's Guide to Dropbox

Table of Contents

Introduction

Welcome and thank you for buying *Dropbox Essentials – The Complete Beginner's Guide to Dropbox!*

This book contains comprehensive guides about the software and its features.

Cloud storage has been a thing of interest in the world of computers in the past few years. Using this technology, users are able to save and access data anywhere and anytime. In addition to real-time access to important information, cloud storage also enables users to securely and reliably create backups of their important files and folders. Moreover, cloud sharing enables multiple users to work on complex projects and collaborative tasks almost *instantaneously*.

Being used by millions of users, *Dropbox* is one of the most popular cloud storage services on the internet. It hosts one of the most reliable, stable, and convenient servers that even free users can enjoy.

Chapter 1 – What is Dropbox?

File storage and ways of storing and retrieving files has always been one of the focal points in computer technology. In turn, administering data transfer and making information accessible from different places by different people became almost synonymous to collaborative work. There was once a time when people used commercial *floppy disks* as the main media when it comes to working with documents, software, and file storage.

As data storage technology evolved, more and more file transfer media were conceived, including *compact discs, USB flash drives,* and *external hard disk drives* (HDDs). In offices, workstations connected in a local network used *shared folders* for collaborative work and seamless file access/transfer. But of course, these methods are still somewhat limited compared to the means of transferring data and information *online.*

Chapter Outline

- *What is Dropbox?*
- *The Brief History of Dropbox*

- *What are the Benefits of Using Dropbox?*

Free flowing information has always been one of the internet's greatest gifts. With the capacity to hold, receive, and send a virtually infinite amount of software; the internet currently serves as the supreme gateway for data and file transfer.

Today, the most practical ways for file transfer and data storage on the internet include sending *attachments* via *e-mail,* using *file hosting websites* to upload and share computer files, and lastly, using *file hosting services* (also known as 'cloud storage service' or 'cyberlocker').

Introduction to Cloud Storage

Dropbox is one of the most popular cloud storage software in the world to date. But first; just *what* is cloud storage and *why* do you need it?

In essence, cloud storage is an online file hosting service that can hold user data such as photos, videos, documents, and other file types. Uploaded files are then made accessible across different platforms such as laptops, tablets, smartphones, and other devices that have internet access.

Additionally, cloud storage systems synchronize stored data in real time – making sure that you always get the most updated version of your files. It is like literally storing your files and data *in the clouds.*

Using physical storage media (flash drives, discs, etc.) is still effective for transferring large amounts of data. However, they are subject to being lost, damaged, theft, or being *forgotten.*

What is Dropbox?

Interestingly, founder *Drew Houston,* said that he developed the idea for Dropbox when he kept forgetting and misplacing his USB flash drive when he was studying at the *Massachusetts Institute of Technology* (MIT). Although there were file hosting services available back then, Houston stated that those services suffered problems and other bugs – especially when handling large file uploads.

Originally intended to help in his academics, Houston developed his own online storage system. It worked so well for his personal use that he instinctively knew everyone else will benefit from it. And after receiving funding from *Y*

Combinator in June 2007, *Dropbox, Inc.* was formed.

So what made Dropbox special when people can still use flash drives, shared network folders, and DVDs to store, share, and receive data? Here are 5 reasons:

1. **Secure Backups** – If you've been using computers for years, you must've experienced the inconvenience of losing data without creating any backups. Everyone knows that computers and storage devices are vulnerable to failures and malfunctions especially without proper maintenance. For instance, bad sectors in hard drives can only get progressively worse until your drive is no longer useable (most hard drives have a healthy lifespan of around 2 years). Additionally, external backups such as flash drives and DVDs can be lost, stolen, or damaged. But if you make it a habit of backing up important files with Dropbox, you will *never* lose your data again – especially since Dropbox is known for having one of the most reliable file hosting servers in the market today.

2. **Increase Computer Speed** – If you have a particularly large *storage quota* for your cloud storage account, you can spare your physical hard drive a generous amount of disk space. Remember that overloading your hard disk can cause slowdowns and *file fragmentation*. This is why storing your data with cloud storage can increase your computer's processing speed, boot time, and performance when running certain applications.

3. **Access your Files from Anywhere** – People enjoy keeping copies of their multimedia files such as photos, videos, eBooks, and other documents in all of their devices. Of course, not all of them are fit for being uploaded in social media accounts. With Dropbox, you can privately store and access your data from your Android device, iPhone, tablet, laptop, and some Symbian phones. Remember that your Dropbox account synchronizes whenever your device is connected to the internet. Additionally, you can grant other users access to your Dropbox folders – making it easy to work with team projects, share photos with distant relatives, and so on.

4. **Easy to Use** – Upon installation, Dropbox installs a location on your computer (the "Dropbox" folder) that you can easily access with your explorer. This makes uploading to your Dropbox account as easy as copying and pasting files. Unlike some other cloud storage services, Dropbox does not have any unnecessary features. Instead, they focus on the security and health of their servers. Furthermore, they ensure that their hosting service is always cross-compatible to the latest gadgets.

5. **Free** – Finally, Dropbox allows users to use their cloud storage service for free. This, of course, has limitations when it comes to the amount of data you can store. A free account is granted a maximum of *2 gigabytes* worth of storage space – enough for keeping hundreds of songs, photos, and some videos. You can also use *'Dropbox for Business'* for a limited time trial.

Valuable data can sometimes be lost when you least expect it. If you're a student, professional, or businessman who relies on computer data for productivity or delivering your work, using Dropbox will make sure you get whatever you need; whenever you need it.

Chapter 2 – Getting Started with Dropbox on your PC

Dropbox delivers the essentials of cloud storage in a fast, functional, and simple way. All you need is a valid e-mail address and you're ready to use Dropbox in any of your devices. But that doesn't mean Dropbox has nothing else *but* the ability to store user files in a cloud-based server.

Users can set certain 'preferences' that can help them manage how Dropbox runs, behaves, and connect to the internet. All these will be discussed in this book. But for now, let's get you started with using Dropbox.

Chapter Outline

- *Getting Started: Step-by-step Dropbox Installation within 10 Minutes*
- *Performing Basic Operations with Dropbox*
- *The Basics of Sharing Files and Folders with Dropbox*

To begin installing Dropbox for your computer, you can download the software for free at https://www.dropbox.com/downloading.

Remember that the file you can get from their website is just the 'downloader' and not the complete installer. Depending on the speed of your internet connection, downloading the necessary files for the Dropbox installation can take anywhere from several seconds to a few minutes.

Signing Up for an Account

If you don't have a Dropbox account yet, you can sign up immediately once the installation completes. After the installation, you will be presented with a small login window. Look for the 'Sign Up' button at the lower left portion of this window to begin registration. You only need to provide a valid e-mail address, your desired username, and password. Just input the appropriate data on the right fields, check "*I agree to the Terms*", and then click on 'Sign Up' to start using Dropbox.

Using Dropbox for the First Time

Upon successful registration, your Dropbox folder is now ready for storing data. If you're unable to find your Dropbox folder, you can find it under 'Places' in Mac OS or under 'Favorites' in Windows.

You can begin saving files into your Dropbox account by dragging and dropping any file or folder into your Dropbox folder. Alternatively, you can use the cut/copy and paste function of your operating system.

To test how fast your Dropbox folder synchronizes with the servers, go ahead and copy multiple files. For the purpose of this tutorial, go ahead and create an empty text file on your Dropbox folder. Name your text document as 'Sample.txt'. Notice that the icons of the files in your Dropbox folder have circle symbols on them:

- **Green/Check Symbol** – This means that the specific file or folder is currently up to date.
- **Blue/Two Arrows Symbol** – This means that the specific file or folder is currently being synchronized.

Once the symbol on a file's icon in your Dropbox folder turns green, it means the latest version of this file is now accessible in all of your devices. Since 'Sample.txt' doesn't contain anything, it should take almost instantaneously for the symbol to become green.

Navigating Dropbox & Working with Individual Files

In your Dropbox folder, you can perform tasks that are similar to your operating system's explorer such as running a virus scan, viewing file properties, printing, and so on. These options can be accessed by right-clicking (Control + Click for Mac) any file's icon and accessing the *'Context Menu'*. Additionally, notice that there are more options in your Dropbox folder files than those stored in other locations.

Go ahead and open the context menu for 'Sample.txt'.

First, you will notice the "**Share Dropbox link**" option. Choosing this option will automatically generate a link to the selected file. This will be confirmed with a notification in your taskbar stating; *"Sharing 'Sample.txt': A link to*

'Sample.txt' has been copied to your clipboard (click to view)."

Clicking this notification will open a window using your default web browser. The selected file will then be visible on this window. Additionally, a link to the selected file is copied to your 'clipboard'. This means you can paste the link to your Dropbox file on any text field (Ctrl + V for Windows or Command + V for Mac).

The next option is **"View on Dropbox.com"**. This option will open the selected folder or the folder where a selected file is located in your web browser.

1. To test this, begin by creating a new folder on your Dropbox folder and rename it to 'SampleFolder'.

2. Next, move 'Sample.txt' in this newly created folder (Drag and drop 'Sample.txt' to 'SampleFolder').

3. Return to your Dropbox folder, open the context menu for 'SampleFolder', and click on 'View on Dropbox.com'.

Note that this will open: https://www.dropbox.com/home/SampleFolder in your default web browser. Take note that there are other interface elements here that are not present in your Dropbox folder. These will be discussed in the next chapter. For now, let's explore the other options in the context menu. Close 'SampleFolder' on your default browser and return to the Dropbox folder.

When opening the context menu for a file, you can see the "**View previous versions**" option. This allows you to restore a file to its former state by undoing changes you've made.

1. To test this feature, go to 'SampleFolder' and open 'Sample.txt'.

2. Next, go ahead and write anything you want and then save your changes.

3. Return to 'SampleFolder'.

4. Open the context menu for 'Sample.txt' and then choose "View previous versions".

This should open *"Revisions – Dropbox"* in your default web browser with the heading; *"Version history of 'Sample.txt'.* In here, you should be able to see versions of 'Sample.txt'. The most updated version of your file is labelled with "(current)" while the previous version is labelled "(oldest)". The file size should also be visible to the right. Of course, it is possible to see several versions of your file depending on how many times you've saved changes.

You should also be able to see which user modified the file and when the changes are made. Finally, you can restore a previous version by selecting it from the list and clicking 'Restore'. Note that only previous versions can be selected and restored. Go ahead and restore the oldest version of 'Sample.txt'. A notification should confirm that the version of 'Sample.txt' in your Dropbox folder has been updated.

Sharing Folders with Dropbox

Lastly, you can share any folder that is saved into your Dropbox account. This is a very important basic feature if you wish to accomplish collaborative work with Dropbox. This is done by opening the context menu for any folder and clicking on "**Share this folder...**"

Important: *Take note that you will need to verify your e-mail address before you can start sharing folders. If this is your first attempt to share a folder, you will be presented with a notification stating that you need to click a verification link from your e-mail. Simply click on 'Send email' and then 'Done' to receive your verification link. Also remember that you can click on "Update email address" in case you can no longer access your e-mail account or if you wish to use another one.*

After clicking on the verification link, you can now share folders with other people. You should be able to see the folder sharing screen when you select "Share this folder..."

1. To test folder sharing, open the context menu for 'SampleFolder' and choose "Share this folder..." (If you selected a folder, this option should replace "View previous versions")

2. This should open the sharing screen in your default web browser. Look for the field labelled with *"Invite members to this folder"* and input the e-mail addresses of the people you wish to share the folder with. Take note

that you can also import contacts from your e-mail account and *Facebook.*

3. You can also add an optional message to your invitation. Remember that this is important if the person you're inviting doesn't know you have a Dropbox account.

There are two more things you need to set if you're using a free account. First, you can select to **allow editors to manage membership of this folder.** Enabling this option will allow other users with 'edit privileges' (also referred to as editors) to invite other people to the shared folder.

Remember that editors can do the following to your Dropbox folder:

- *Leave or cancel access to your shared folder*
- *View and modify folder contents*
- *View the list of members and their privileges*
- *Send e-mails to other members*
- *Modify member privileges*
- *Manage invitations*
- *Invite or remove members to the folder (with the exception of the owner)*

Lastly, you can assign new editors whenever inviting new people to your folder or by managing your members. By default, the new people you invite are granted edit privileges. To change this, look for the 'can edit' option and set it to 'can view'.

Chapter 3 – Dropbox Settings & Preferences

Users of Dropbox are allowed to set certain preferences to control how the software runs and behaves in the background. Additionally, there are *account settings* wherein you can set your personal e-mail address, your account photo, contacts, and other account/security settings.

After installing Dropbox on your computer, you can do this in *2* ways:

1. Through the Dropbox *taskbar icon*

2. By going to www.dropbox.com, clicking on your account name (upper-right corner of the screen), and then clicking on 'Settings'

Chapter Outline

- *How to Set your Dropbox Preferences*

The easiest way to start controlling how your Dropbox runs is through the taskbar icon. To begin, right-click on the Dropbox icon in your taskbar/system tray (small, blue open box) and click on the settings button (gear with an arrow down). Next, click on "**Preferences...**" to open the Dropbox Preferences window.

Setting Dropbox Preferences

There are **5** main tabs in the Preferences window.

In the **General** tab, you can set the basic system settings such as *"Show desktop notifications"*, *"Start Dropbox on system startup"*, and *"Language"*.

1. **Show desktop notifications** – If you want to receive desktop notifications whenever Dropbox completes a task or has other updates, enable this option. If you think that desktop notifications can distract you or impede your work in any way, deselect this option.

2. **Start Dropbox on system startup** – If you want to automatically start Dropbox and synchronize your files whenever you start your computer, enable this option. It is recommended for you to allow Dropbox to run during system startup. This ensures that your files will always be synchronized in real time.

3. **Language** – Lastly, you can set a specific language as the default language for Dropbox. Simply look and select your desired language.

In the **Account** tab, you can set the location of your Dropbox folder on your computer. You can also set which folders will be synchronized and 'unlink' a Dropbox account on your computer.

1. **Location** – Clicking on the "**Move**" button will allow you to specify a new location for Dropbox on your computer. Remember that this will also move any existing files and folders in your current Dropbox folder.

2. **Selective sync** – Click this to choose which folders in your Dropbox folder will be synchronized. Remember that subfolders can also be individually selected. Simply click on the arrow on

3. **Account Linking** – Click on "**Unlink This Dropbox...**" if you want to disconnect your Dropbox account with your computer. Remember that this will disable any further synchronization, but will *not delete* the files and folders stored locally.

In the **Import** tab, you can set your upload preferences for *photos* and *videos* whenever you connect a mobile device or other external media. Remember that you can set newly connected devices to automatically upload to your Dropbox account by changing your 'AutoPlay' settings for Windows. This will be discussed in the *next chapter (Automatically Upload Data from Media & External Devices)*.

1. **Camera Upload** – There are two options when setting camera uploads; *photos only* and *photos and videos*. Keep in mind that videos are generally larger than photos. If you want to save more space on your Dropbox account, leave this option to 'photos only'.

2. **Screenshots** – Enabling the option "**Share screenshots using Dropbox**" will automatically save new desktop screenshots (*Ctrl + Prt Scn* for Windows) to your Dropbox folder. Take note that if you enable this option, you can no longer paste the screenshot on an image editor (Paint, etc.).

In the **Bandwidth** tab, you can set specific bandwidth usage of Dropbox whenever uploading or downloading data. You can also enable synchronization via LAN.

1. **Download Rate** – Use this to set specific bandwidth usage limitations whenever downloading new data. Keep in mind that in slower internet connections, Dropbox can sometimes prevent users from accessing the internet when synchronizing. If you have a slow internet connection, consider limiting your download rate to 50-100 KB/s.

2. **Upload Rate** – Use this to set specific bandwidth usage limitations whenever uploading new data. For the same reasons above, leave this option to *"Limit automatically"* or set specific upload rate limitations. Take note that selecting "Limit automatically" will allow Dropbox to cap uploads to 75% of your upload speed capacity.

3. **Enable LAN sync** – Enabling this option will allow you to synchronize your Dropbox with other computers connected to the same local area network. Remember that the other computers should also have Dropbox accounts with access privileges to your Dropbox folder. If you disable this, your Dropbox client will

have to use the Dropbox servers to relay new data to other computers.

Lastly, you can use *proxy servers* by setting the correct information on the **Proxies** tab. For new users, it is recommended to leave this option to "**Auto-**detect". This is because improperly setting proxy servers can prevent Dropbox from accessing the internet.

1. **No Proxy** – This will disable Dropbox from using proxy servers to connect to the internet. This can sometimes solve connectivity issues with Dropbox.

2. **Auto-detect** – This will allow Dropbox to detect and use specific proxy settings that maybe required by your internet service provider. If you're not experiencing any connection problems with Dropbox, choose this option.

3. **Manual** – Remember that this is recommended for advanced users only. Using a proxy server allows Dropbox to bypass a corporate firewall or certain connectivity limitations set by your network administrator.

Dropbox supports the proxy protocols; *HTTP, SOCKS4,* and *SOCKS5*. If you need to use a proxy server, simply input the proxy server's URL in the 'Server' field along with the required port value. If your proxy server requires a valid username and password, select *"Proxy server requires a password"* and then input the correct data in the appropriate fields.

Chapter 4 – Using Dropbox in Your Life

Dropbox saves anyone the trouble of synchronizing files such as photos, videos, and work documents in different locations. With Dropbox, you can easily create and share multiple folders for "Family Photos", "Work Documents", "Business", and anything else you require. If you are using *Dropbox for Business,* you will have a Dropbox folder for both your personal data and work data. But you can also create separate shared folders with a free account.

Remember that only one Dropbox account can be linked to a computer at any given time. This means that if you are using 2 or more Dropbox accounts, you will have to unlink the current account first and then login your other account. Additionally, you will have to create a new location for your other account's Dropbox folder. To save you from this inconvenience, you can easily create different folders on *one* Dropbox account with different sharing options.

Chapter Outline

- *How to Manage your Shared Folders*
- *How to Automatically Upload Files from External Media & Devices*

In Chapter 2, you learned about how to create and share folders with other users. Additionally, you learned how to use *selective sync* to set which folders will be synchronized and which will not. In this section, you will learn how to create **3** separate folders for your family, work, and business.

Gathering Contacts

Remember that you need e-mail addresses before you can share folders. If you haven't imported your contacts to your Dropbox account yet, you can import your contacts from Gmail, Yahoo, and Facebook by following the instructions in Chapter 2 – *Sharing Folders with Dropbox* and clicking on 'Import Contacts' when inputting an e-mail address.

Creating New Shared Folders

An alternative to creating new folders directly on your Dropbox folder and sharing that folder is to create a new shared folder at https://www.dropbox.com/share (make sure you are logged in on your computer). Notice that the link above will open the sharing options on your default web browser. Use the following instructions to create your **business** and **family** folders.

1. On the sharing screen, click on "**New shared folder**"

2. Select "*I'd like to create and share a new folder*" and click 'Next'.

3. Name your first folder 'Business' and click 'Next'.

4. Notice that this opens the sharing options for your work folder. In the "*Invite members to this folder*" field, input the e-mail addresses of your business partners/colleagues (press 'enter' to insert multiple e-mail addresses).

5. You may include an optional message to your invitation. Make sure you specify if your

contacts can edit the contents of your folder (refer to Chapter 2 – *Sharing Folders with Dropbox*). You can also change these settings later on in this chapter.

6. Click on 'Share Folder' to create your new folder.

7. Repeat the steps to create your 'Family' folder. Just change step 4 to the e-mail addresses of your relatives whom you want to share the folder with.

Upon receiving and your invitation, these people will now have access to your 'Work' and 'Family' folders. Make sure you notify them so that they accept your invitation as soon as possible.

After creating your folders, you may now upload any content you wish to share with other people. For example, show your holiday pictures to your parents in your 'Family' folder or share your presentation with your business in your 'Business' folder. With a little creativity, you can always find new ideas to enjoy the seamless interconnectivity of shared Dropbox folders.

Also remember that if your family's devices and computers are connected via LAN, make sure you use "**Enable LAN sync**" in the Bandwidth settings on your Dropbox preferences. This will enable your data to be synchronized much faster using your LAN connection.

Setting Folder Options

Next, you'll need to verify your members and their privileges to your folder. In the sharing options, you should be able to see the two new folders you've created along with the time when they were last modified. Click on 'Options' located to the right-most side of the screen (aligned to the specific folder). This will open the 'Shared folder options'.

In the shared folder options, you can see the list of members who can access your folder along with their privileges. Make sure to specify which members are able to edit the contents of your folder. You can also remove a member by clicking the 'X' button to the right.

Lastly, you can 'unshare' a folder by clicking the 'Unshare folder' button at the bottom of the shared folder options window. This is useful if you accidentally shared a private folder. You may also leave a folder by clicking the 'Leave folder' button and then confirming your decision.

Creating a Personal Work Folder

Using shared folders to synchronize your work with a team for big projects is a good way to increase productivity with Dropbox. However, Dropbox also enables you to synchronize your documents from your work computer to your home computer. All you have to do is to create a new folder on your Dropbox folder and rename it as 'Personal/Work'.

Automatically Upload Data from Media & External Devices

In Windows, you can automatically upload files from external devices such as Audio CDs, Cameras, and so on by changing the 'AutoPlay' settings. These settings can be changed by going to Control Panel → Hardware and Sound → AutoPlay (For Windows 7 and Windows 8).

First, make sure you select *"Use AutoPlay for all media and devices"* located at the top of the screen. Under 'Media' and 'Devices', you should see a list of media and all the devices you've ever connected to your computer (CD, Mixed Content, Apple *iPhone, Blu-ray* disc movie, etc.).

To automatically upload videos and photos to your Dropbox account, choose "*Import photos and videos using Dropbox*" from the dropdown menu located to the right of your selected media/device.

Important: *Remember that files from your external media will only be automatically uploaded using this method whenever you connect them to your computer.*

Chapter 5 – Store More with Dropbox

Sharing your data in real time with Dropbox is an excellent way to boost collaborative effort and to enjoy memorable moments with the people that matter. But there is more to Dropbox than just cloud storage. This chapter covers how to maximize your experience with Dropbox.

Chapter Outline

- *How to Get More Space with Dropbox for Free*

To make your data always readily available, you can download and install Dropbox for your *Android, iPad, iPhone,* or *Blackberry* device.

Simply go to this website (https://www.dropbox.com/mobile)

Select your device type, and click on 'Install Directions'. Alternatively, you can click on *"Text to my phone"* or *"Email to my device"* to download Dropbox directly from your mobile device.

Getting More Space

One problem with the free basic account is that you are limited to *2.00 GB* upload quota. One way to increase your save space is to upgrade to "*Dropbox* Pro". For paid accounts, you get *1 TB* or *1,000 GB* save data. Remember that this will cost you $9.99 per month for the additional space and sharing controls.

However, basic accounts can still obtain more space by *completing Dropbox 'quests'* or through *'referrals'*.

First, you can obtain **250 MB** more space on your basic account by completing 5 out of 7 tasks found here: https://www.dropbox.com/gs

If you've successfully followed all the steps in this book, you would've already done 5-6 out of 7 tasks (*installing Dropbox on your computer, sharing a folder with friends or colleagues, etc.*). This means you should be able to obtain your 250 bonus space by now.

How Referrals Work

Dropbox also grants basic users a maximum of *16 GB* additional space for referrals. First, you can go to the referral page (https://www.dropbox.com/referrals) and invite your friends and colleagues via e-mail. Additionally, you can share your referral link found under *"More ways to invite your friends"* in social media websites. Simply copy the given link and paste it so that others can see.

For every friend who fulfills the referral requirements, you will get 500 MB additional space (1 GB for Dropbox Pro accounts). All in all, you can enjoy *18 GB* storage space for your free account with just referrals.

Remember that people should *use* your referral link to download Dropbox and create their account using the desktop application in order for the referral to count. It doesn't matter even if your friend or colleague uses a different e-mail address. As long as he/she uses your link and signs up with the desktop application, you will still get your 500 MB additional space.

Conclusion

Thank you and I hope you enjoyed reading *Dropbox Essentials – The Complete Beginner's Guide to Dropbox.*

I hope this book was able to help you understand the basics of Dropbox and put them all in application.

Printed in Great Britain
by Amazon